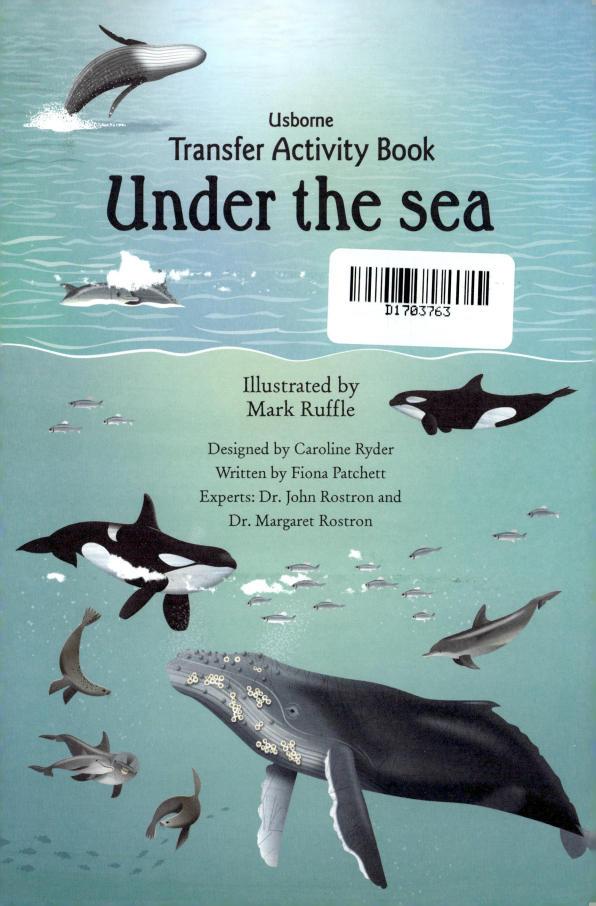

How to use the transfers

At the front of this book you'll find sheets of transfers. Using a pencil or ballpoint pen, you can add these transfers to the scenes on the right-hand pages of the book. First, take the transfer sheets out of their pocket and find one with the symbol that matches the symbol on the page you want to work on. Most sheets contain the transfers for three scenes. Carefully remove the backing sheet.

To use the transfers, position one of the little pictures over the place you want it to go in the scene.

Use a pencil or ballpoint pen to scribble firmly on the front of the sheet all over the picture. Take care not to touch the pictures around it.

When you have completely covered the transfer, gently lift off the transfer sheet to reveal the new picture.

Pack the scenes with lots of darting fish and scuttling sea creatures.

Welcome to an underwater world

It's a different world under the sea. There are huge mountains and valleys, grassy meadows and forests of tall sea plants. Some parts are warm and others are icy cold. Some are shallow and others are so deep, only a few people have ever been there.

The world's seas and oceans are teeming with an amazing array of fish and sea creatures of all different shapes and sizes, from mighty whales and lumbering walruses to gliding jellyfish and tiny barnacles. Find out more about them on the pages of this book.

Usborne Quicklinks

For links to websites where you can see dolphins, turtles, sharks and all sorts of other sea creatures, go to usborne.com/Quicklinks and type in the keywords 'under the sea transfers'. Please read our online safety guidelines at the Usborne Quicklinks website. Children should be supervised online.

Coral reefs

In warm, shallow waters, coral reefs are bustling with all sorts of bright fish. Fill this reef with transfers of even more fish and sea creatures.

Put this manta ray swooping above the coral.

This lionfish has poisonous spines.

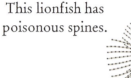

Reef shark

Put these Moorish idol fish close to the coral.

Arrange these yellow tangs so they can clean a turtle's shell.

Add some butterflyfish.

Green turtles swim above the reef.

Emperor angelfish dart in and out of the coral.

A parrotfish pecks at the coral.

Arrange this blue sea star clinging to the coral.

Mandarin fish

Put these clownfish near the others.

Icy waters

The Arctic is always cold. A thick layer of ice covers most of the ocean, but underneath, the water is full of life.

Put these chunks of ice floating on the surface.

Arrange these bearded seals in the sea and on the ice.

A walrus uses its tusks to pull itself onto the ice.

Add these walruses to the scene.

Place this polar bear swimming just below the surface.

These are narwhals. They have long, pointed tusks.

A lion's mane jellyfish

Ringed seals chasing fish to eat

Put these beluga whales under the water.

Squid

Arctic cod

Tiny sea creatures called krill will make a tasty meal for the huge bowhead whale.

Greenland halibut

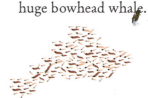

Mangrove swamp

Mangrove trees grow along tropical seashores. They have long, deep roots, which form thick, underwater forests. Lots of creatures live around the tangled roots.

Mudskippers use their fins to crawl over the mud.

Add these skittering frogs leaping across the surface.

A dog-faced water snake swims across the surface.

Put this male fiddler crab near the other one.

Arrange these hooded oysters on the mangrove roots.

Rainbow sardines

Horseshoe crabs swimming underwater

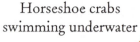

A baby shark shelters between the tree roots.

An electric ray hides at the bottom of the sea, waiting for crabs to eat.

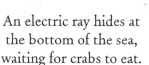

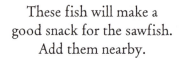

Sawfish

These fish will make a good snack for the sawfish. Add them nearby.

Put these mud crabs on the seabed.

Dolphins and whales

Dolphins and whales love to splash and play in the water. They breathe air at the surface, then dive deep to hunt for food.

A dolphin plays in the waves alongside the boat.

A whale throws its tail up above the water as it dives.

A Cuvier's beaked whale leaping

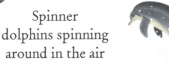

Spinner dolphins spinning around in the air

Water sprays up as this dolphin breathes out through a blowhole on its head.

This orca is a type of dolphin. Put it under the water.

Arrange these dolphins so they're poking their heads out of the water.

Animals called barnacles grow on whales. Add these to the others on the humpback whale.

Herring

A dolphin hunts underwater for fish to eat.

Humpback whale

A baby bottlenose dolphin swimming with its mother

On the seabed

All sorts of creatures make their home at the bottom of the sea. They live on the sandy seabed or hide between the rocks and coral.

Put this sea pen next to the other ones.

Put more mussels on the rocks.

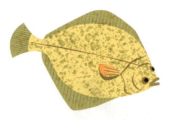

A flounder tries to hide on the sandy seabed.

Find a place between the rocks where this lobster can hide.

Dragonets

Put these scorpionfish near a bobbit worm.

Mantis shrimp

This bobbit worm is ready to snap its wide jaws around a fish.

Place this octopus by the rocks, waiting for fish to grab and eat.

Put it poking out of the sand.

Angel shark

King scallops swimming through water

Deep, dark sea

In some places, the sea is very deep and dark. If you explored in a submarine, you'd find underwater fountains called black smokers, and strange creatures living there.

Hatchetfish

Vampire squid

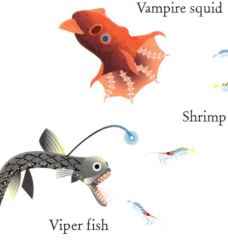

Shrimp

A gulper eel's glowing tail attracts shrimp. It scoops them up in one big gulp.

Dumbo octopus

Viper fish

This anglerfish has a glowing lure above its mouth to attract fish.

Arrange these yeti crabs on a black smoker.

Put these unlucky fish close to the anglerfish's sharp teeth.

A deep sea cucumber swims above a black smoker.

Put this deep sea vent octopus on the seabed.

Add these zoarcid fish flitting between the giant tubeworms.

These giant tubeworms are taller than a person.

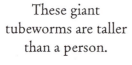

Shipwreck

Divers are exploring the wreck of a ship that sank hundreds of years ago. If they're lucky, they may find some treasure.

Jellyfish

Put these divers near the shipwreck.

A moray eel hides in the shipwreck.

A sea krait swimming through the coral

An old dagger lies on the seabed.

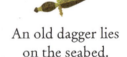

Coral trout

Zebra fish flit in and out of the shipwreck.

Place this old vase where a diver can find it.

Clown triggerfish

Put this treasure chest on the seabed.

Seagrass meadow

In shallow seas, seagrass grows in large meadows on the seabed. Lots of sea creatures live there too.

A spine-bellied sea snake slinks through the seagrass.

This is a dugong. Put it munching the seagrass in the distance.

Add these feather stars to the seabed.

Put this chocolate chip starfish on the seabed.

Ornate eagle ray

A pipefish hides in the seagrass.

Golden trevally

A seahorse swimming

Baby fish shelter in the seagrass.

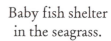

This seahorse is clinging to some seagrass.

Put these scallops on the seagrass leaves.

Sea hares

Island life

The remote Galapagos Islands lie in the Pacific Ocean. They are home to many sea creatures that are not found anywhere else.

A Galapagos sea lion resting on the beach

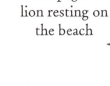

Put this flightless cormorant on the rocks near the beach, where it can dry its wings.

Arrange these Sally Lightfoot crabs near the others.

A Galapagos green turtle looks for food on the seabed.

A flightless cormorant diving through the water

A spotted eagle ray swimming

A Galapagos penguin swims underwater.

Put this spotted eagle ray jumping out of the water to escape a hungry shark.

King angelfish

Razorfish

Scalloped hammerhead shark

This red-lipped batfish uses its fins to walk along the seabed.

Place these marine iguanas underwater.

First published in 2020 by Usborne Publishing Ltd., Usborne House, 83-85 Saffron Hill, London EC1N 8RT England. usborne.com Copyright © 2020 Usborne Publishing Ltd. The name Usborne and the devices 🎈 🎈 are Trade Marks of Usborne Publishing Ltd. All rights reserved. No part of this publication may be reproduced, stored in a retrieval system, or transmitted in any form or by any means, electronic, mechanical, photocopying, recording or otherwise without the prior permission of Usborne Publishing Ltd. UKE

The websites recommended at Usborne Quicklinks are regularly reviewed but Usborne Publishing is not responsible and does not accept liability for the availability or content of any website other than its own, or for any exposure to harmful, offensive or inaccurate material which may appear on the Web. Usborne Publishing will have no liability for any damage or loss caused by viruses that may be downloaded as a result of browsing the sites it recommends.